PARENT BAILOUT

PARENT BAILOUT

The Bailout That Is
Really Crippling America

Dr. Charlotte Rainey Green

outskirtspress

DENVER, COLORADO

Carl and Icy Rainey
A model worth reflecting

I would like to dedicate this book to my parents, Carl and Icy Rainey. God blessed me with parents who accepted the responsibility of instructing and nurturing children. Because my parents successfully performed their duties, other social systems were effective in collaborating with my parents to successfully fulfill their responsibilities. I am one of fifteen children, and we all are productive citizens in our society. We all give back to our communities in some capacity and contribute to making them a better place to live.

Carl and Icy Rainey understood that although they had many responsibilities in life, none was greater than the responsibility of parenting. They lived Deuteronomy 6:7 and taught their children truths of our heavenly Father. They were able to instruct because they were there in the home listening, feeding, teaching, and giving us what we needed emotionally, so we did not need to get our physical and emotional needs met elsewhere.

When I was working on my dissertation, I initially used the term "raised" when talking about nurturing and teaching children. The computer software program I used to type my paper did not like the term "raise" in the context of discussing children. It recognized it as a correlation to crops. That was interesting to me and prompted me to think about what it really means to "raise" children. Although we commonly use the term when referring to instructing children, it is not clear what that term means. Does "raise" mean just to feed to make grow, or does it mean to instruct? I think the vagueness of the term is part of the problem in families. Many parents are feeding and clothing, but not instructing. I think my typing program wanted me to use the term "instruct" or "teach" when referring to children because the term "raising" was not clear enough. It did not provide the explicit action needed to indentify what the verb was doing. I think when we talk about parental responsibility; we need to be clearer in articulating what that means. We need to talk about what the "raising" and the "teaching" look like.

Carl and Icy Rainey made a priority to both "raise" and "instruct" their children. I cannot remember one single morning when I did not wake to a hot breakfast. If I went to school hungry, it was out of my youthful foolishness for rejecting the homemade biscuits and hot cereal prepared for me daily in exchange for a cold Little Debbie oatmeal pie. In the "raising" of their children, our parents made sure we had what we needed before we went to school every morning. Carl and Icy Rainey verbally gave us instruction, but the greatest instruction came from the model they displayed before us. Our dad modeled how a husband is to love his wife, lead his family, and provide for his children. Our mom modeled how a wife respects her husband, communicates with her children, and sacrifices for her family. My siblings and I were blessed. I was taught that your actions follow your beliefs. I think that people say what they want others to believe about them, but they actually live what they really believe. Thank you, Mom and Dad, for not just talking about what you believe. Thank you for living what you believe and honoring your responsibilities as parents. Your life serves as a model to your children and others, and the term "parent bailout" would not exist if all parents were like you.

TABLE OF CONTENTS

ANGRY PEOPLE

It was August 5, 2010. I turned from one cable news channel to the other and saw the same sense of frustration and anger. At first, I thought it was propaganda of certain channels, but as I flipped from station to station, and as I turned from channel to channel, the tone was the same. The message was the same, regardless of each channel's personal twist of the story. As I sat in my bed watching the nine o'clock news to catch up on current events, I found myself speechless and bothered. As I engaged in my normal routine of winding down before bed, I found myself restless.

It was fall of 2010; I would describe the climate of America as frustrated. Individuals expressed great dissatisfaction with the expansion of government and appeared to be unsettled with the direction of America's future. Media coverage of the 2010 midterm elections revealed anger and discontentment among thousands, if not millions, of American people. Listening to the language of politicians, political analysis, and citizens, I quickly realized the "united" America that we all love was in jeopardy. What was happening? What was compromising the unity in our community?

High unemployment rates, the expansion of government, corporate bailouts, government spending, and the decrease of worth in the American dollar were all concerns prompting passionate discussions among Americans. The American culture was so disgruntled during the fall of 2010 a new political party emerged. The birth of the Tea Party was some individuals' answer to address the multiple issues that angered Americans. With a stated goal to implement practices to guide Americans to become more fiscally sound and responsible, the Tea Party materialized and modified the political climate once dominated by Democrats and Republicans.

What was the source of a frustration and discontent so intense that a new political party emerged? What was at the heart of anger so deep that it made it difficult for some to display respect to the highest office in our country? What was the reason that as I sat in my bed to watch the news, I felt a sadness and uneasiness new to me? What was happening? I think the answer is the fear of an unbalanced country, because everyone knows an unbalanced anything falls.

What I do not understand is why unbalanced is unacceptable in some aspects of our society, but expected in others. If we all know an unbalanced anything falls, then should any imbalance be tolerated? How did we become a society where corporate or bank bailouts anger society, but parent bailouts are expected?

BAILOUTS

"Government Bailouts" was the term for fall 2010. Banks needed bailing out, corporations needed bailing out, and mortgages needed bailing out. Bailouts can be defined as one entity coming to the aid and helping another entity. The idea of the government coming to the aid of other entities of our society seemed to be a new initiative, but the reality is that bailouts are not new to America and are an essential component to what makes our society balanced. You see, America operates as a functionalist society, and bailouts are an important element of functionalist societies. Although the term "bailout" is new, the concept of one social structure assisting another troubled social structure is not pioneering. The term "bailout" describes the social attitude of a functionalist society.

According to deMarrais and LeCompte (1999), a functionalist society argues that society operates like the human body, and all societies possess basic functions which they must carry out to survive. Functionalists believe that if one socializing institution is not fulfilling its function, another will take over its role to maintain the equilibrium of the society (deMarrais and LeCompte). Successful civilizations are created when all the various components of society work together to form a union of services and support to meet the needs of its people. Functionalists believe that society is made up of several social support structures, such as government, school systems, medical industry, private sectors, religious organizations, and families. The collaboration of the various support structures provides a social system that is functional and secure for the citizens within the society. Security within a functionalist society occurs because each support entity takes an interest in the other to ensure all entities are successful. If one of the support elements struggles, functionalists believe it is the job of the other support element to aid the struggling system until it is healthy and functioning independently. Bailouts are simply one support entity coming to the aid of the struggling support entity, because all entities need to be successful to maintain a healthy society. Functionalists believe that the strength of a society is the strength of each individual support system, which makes the success of all social system essential to a successful culture. Therefore, when one support system is not healthy, another support system comes to its aid until the suffering support system is healthy.

I agree that a functionalist system supports healthy societies and fosters success for all social functions, but I also understand the burden placed on the support system providing the support and the danger placed on the support system receiving the support. There is a risk of further weakening of the unhealthy support system if too much support is provided. Actually, there is a danger of weakening both systems because of the burden placed on one system and the possible enabling placed on the other. The appropriate amount of support is critical to maintain the success of all social systems.

An example of American society balancing itself through interdependent relationships among support systems would be the government support system helping the family support system through government assistance programs. Business support systems support school support systems through private grants and mentoring programs. Religious support systems support family support systems through family counseling and other family-building programs. Medical and government support systems join to offer support to both schools and family support systems with affordable clinics, school grants and programs, and medical programs for families. Social support systems coming to the aid of a weak support system in America is not a new idea; interdependent relationships among American social support systems has occurred throughout American history. The originality of this era is the increase of discussion regarding the scale of support and the balancing of the social systems.

In looking at the various support systems during the year of 2010, one of the main issues was that private support systems were struggling and the government support system came to the aid to maintain an effective society. I think there are two alarming factors that frustrated America and fueled the frustration displayed in the 2010 midterm elections. The social support aid commonly known as the bailouts of 2009-2010 included government coming to the aid of certain private support systems. Americans were alarmed because private support systems are private, and they have their own agendas that are not subject to public or government approval. Bailouts for private sectors are complicated because using taxpayers' funds to help profit-based and private organizations is difficult for individuals to accept. However, private businesses are an important social structure and cannot fail. What do you do when they struggle?

The second alarming factor is the amount of funds provided. The funds provided to stop mortgage foreclosures, save private businesses, increase employment, and arouse public spending contributed to an increase in the American deficit. Although American overspending did not begin in 2009, government spending combined with the bailouts created an unprecedented displeasure with federal government among many Americans.

People felt like the amount of funding and the types of bailouts were creating a weak fiscal system and an enlargement of the government support system. The American people were responding to a fear of an unbalanced social system during the 2010-midterm elections. Many individuals were frustrated because they felt like government had too much power and was weakening private support systems. The Tea Party, founded on the frustration of big government and overspending, elected officials who did not support a system of government bailouts and won positions in Congress during the 2010 midterm election. Many individuals felt like the government support system was becoming too big and damaging to private businesses. The danger of an unbalanced system created a frustrated America. Functionalism was working in American government during government bailouts of 2009. Functionalism continues to be a personality of our country and occurs in many social entities within the United States. Are they all upsetting? Do all bailouts generate discussions among Americans because of the fear of an unbalanced system? Lets talk about schools. It is common knowledge that the family structure is a structure in America that is constantly changing, but many would argue that it is a structure that is consistently weakening. Who is aiding this struggling structure? I would say government and the public school system. According to deMarrais and LeCompte, today's society depends on schools to provide functions formerly performed by the social system called the family. I call this form of social support the "parent bailout."

PARENT BAILOUT

It is not uncommon to hear Americans complain about the amount of aid the government gives to struggling families because of the fear of an unbalanced system. I have heard Americans say that the unbalanced support only weakens an already struggling family and exhaust government resources. Balancing the support system is important to people, but for some reason, the imbalance between the school support system and family support system is accepted. What about the support school systems are required to give families? Is it exhausting school resources? Funding is given to schools to assist, but what about unintended consequences? Today's school systems are required to implement various family programs to address issues that were once the responsibility of the family (deMarrais & LeCompte). Schools assist with children's personal care, meals, emotional support, and supplies necessary for school. The government has given school systems additional funds to address the family issues within the school system. School support systems have come to the aid of family support systems for many years, creating a parent bailout.

The parent bailout does not generate the same level of frustration in the American people as private sector bailouts. Why is that? Long-term bailouts do not work because they weaken all support systems involved. The parent bailout has an unintended consequences of forcing schools to operate out of their intended purpose. Although the school is a logical place to provide support to the family, to make it part of the schools permanant responsibility compromises the intergrity of what schools were designed to do. School systems are not designed to handle the responsibilities for family support systems for an extended period as it stretches their resources. Family structures become weaker as the dependency on school systems to provide various family service increases. The imbalance between school systems and family support systems weakens the school and the family. According to Murphy (2006), schools were designed to educate children and give them the tools to be productive citizens for the welfare of our nation. Today, schools are responsible for more than providing education because they have taken on family responsibilities with the parent bailout. The parent bailout has compromised the level of academic rigor that occurs in schools, because schools have to address issues that formerly were addressed in the home. The parent bailout has weakened school systems and given parents a venue not to take full responsibility for the success of their children. School systems should be collaborative partners with parents, with both structures fulfilling their functions. Parents should hold schools accountable to educate their children, and schools should be able to depend on parents to provide the family structure necessary for success in life.

People want balance in our society because the imbalance is dangerous. Americans understand that imbalance in business can create an economic problem that will hinder the core of America. One of the statements heard during the 2010 midterm election was "the destroying of American capitalistic economy starts with big government." Individuals interviewed by news personalities expressed the fear of America losing the fundamental principles of America. I find it interesting that the capitalistic society is considered the foundational anchor to America. Why is it not family structure? Which is more damaging to a society, the decrease of private sector businesses in our country or the deterioration of the family? The economy has created great debate and uncertainty regarding America's future, but the parent bailout is the bailout that is really crippling America.

THE EXPENSE OF
PARENT BAILOUT

Parent bailouts exhaust government and school resources and lessen the responsibility of families. Few would argue the financial burden parent bailout places on government, but there is minimal discussion on how the parent bailout has exhausted resources and added non-academic responsibility to school systems. Public school systems were created with the goal of educating individuals to be productive citizens and contribute to the society. American schools were designed to produce individuals who could read in order to obey the laws, lead their families, and contribute to society for the welfare of the nation (Murphy). Thomas Jefferson understood the critical need to have an educated society when he stated, "Whenever people are well-informed, they can be trusted with their own government." John F. Kennedy also expressed the importance of an educated society when he said, "Remember that our nation's first great leaders were also our first great scholars." No one argues the critical role education plays in a successful society. However, do actions support that belief system? Does our society compromise the quality of education given to our children because of the additional responsibilities given to the system? Can a school system educate children and provide the emotional support previously provided in the home and continue to be effective at educating students?

The education of students is complex because of the various variables that affect a child's academic performance. School systems that focus on student achievement understand that other variables influence student achievement and implement various practices that help children get their basic needs met. Schools have to focus on the overall needs of children in the process of educating the child. Maslow's hierarchy of needs is a fundamental framework for educators, and teachers understand that a child's basic needs must be met before learning occurs. When a child comes to school without their basic needs fulfilled, the school addresses the student's needs. The number of children who come to school lacking basic needs increases year after year, and many parents have come to expect the school to meet some of the basic needs for their children.

Now, I am not saying that the school should not assist children. Maslow tells us that kids do not learn if they do not have their basic needs met. I am saying that when schools have to focus a great amount of attention to non-academic issues, it compromises the quality of education. Let me give you an example: Imagine you own a factory that designs boots. You have established yourself as a leading boot designer and have a reputation of providing quality boots. For company effectiveness, you collaborate with a shoestring company. Collaborating with this company helps your factory to focus on quality, detail, and resources for the development of excellent boots. You have a great relationship with the shoestring company, and you need them to produce a quality shoestring in order for the boot to have the desired quality. One day the shoestring company asks you to start making the shoestrings due to problems within their company. You cannot say no because you need the shoestrings for the boots. You get additional funds to assist in making shoestrings. As time passes, the boot company is expected to make more and more shoestrings, the shoestring company expects the boot company to make quality shoestrings, and the quality of the actual boots is decreasing. Not only is the actual boot decreasing in quality, but also the shoestrings created at the boot company are not as good as those created at the shoestring company. Because the shoestring company is now looking to the boot company to make both, they are critical of the quality of the shoestrings, boots, and the overall product. Boot sales decline as customers discover other boots that have strong shoestring companies as partners, and everyone talks about the poor quality of the boots of the company that is producing both the shoestring and the boot.

The boot company represents the school system, the shoestring company represents the parents, and the actual boot represents the student achievement. The boot company was successful as long as it was operating for its intended purpose. The company was not as productive with the additional responsibilities. School systems were designed to educate children. Individuals study education as a profession and receive training in teaching children; they are not trained in all the additional responsibilities that are now placed on them. Moreover, just as the boot company could not perform to its full potential when it had to produce shoestrings, school systems cannot operate to their full potential when they have to parent children. The additional responsibilities added to schools include items that historically were addressed in the home. Since many homes are struggling with parenting and providing for children, the schools are forced to meet the emotional and physical needs of children. With increasing intellectual competitiveness in the global job market and American schools forced to focus on the physical and emotional needs of students, our school system is slowly falling behind in its goal of producing qualified students who are prepared to be productive citizens who can lead our country and compete with the rest of the world.

The cost of failing schools is immense and affects the American economy in a negative way. The expense of parent bailout has multiple negative influences ranging from weaker family support systems to a failing economy. The expense of parent bailout ends with a failing economy, but it often starts with a failing family. Throughout history, there has been no stronger institute for the American society than the family. The tribal aspect of society has been around for centuries. When we look at the influence a single family can have in American society, we can easily see its tremendous impact. Think about major companies and individual contributions that have root in a family structure. How many major American corporations started with a family? How many potential American companies never became companies because of a lack of family empowerment? The parent bailout weakens the family structure and exhausts the structure that is assisting the family, resulting in an imbalance of social responsibility.

Few will argue the point that strengthening families would make a stronger society, but how does that happen. If a failing economy begins with failing families, how do we go back to that foundational structure of our society and empower the family to function in its full capacity? Strengthening the family will strengthen schools, and strengthening schools will strengthen our economy. Often time parents are feeding and clothing, but not instructing. Although in the minority, there are some parents who look for others to feed and cloth their children. An effective parent provides their children with what they need physically and emotionally. There are multiple strategies used to strengthen the family structure that assist parents in meeting both the physcial and emotional needs of their children. This book continues with a discussion focused on emotional support because the benefit is not alway as obvious as the physical support. What does healthy emotional support look like in effective parenting? As you turn the pages of this book, you will engage in a narraitve discussion on parenting styles and the influence those styles have on child development. Understanding parenting styles equips the parent to have strategic interaction and provide emotional support.

Like many parents, I am a parent who attempts to provide my children with both the physically and emotional support. I am far from perfect, but understanding the various parenting styles have helped me correct some of my parenting mistakes. I am a better parent because I understand the influence of my interaction. I pray to God everyday to give me wisdom, because parenting is the greatest and scariest responsiblity I have.

I am also an educator and I have learned the connection between strategic parenting and high student achievement, which is what prompted me to write this book. As you continue reading this book, I pray that you go through a process that I went through that includes self reflection and gaining knowledge. Lets proceed with a discussion on the three major parenting styles (authoritarian, authoritative, and permissive).

There is a fourth style called neglectful. This book does not talk about neglectful parenting, because that involves not providing the physical needs of a child. Because you are reading this book, it likely that you are not a neglectful parent. You are probably a parent that makes the best decisions with the information you have and most likely have authoritative, authoritarian, or permissive parenting characteristics.

As you read, reflect on your behavior and see if you can determine your dominate style.

EMPOWERING FAMILIES THROUGH STRATEGIC PARENTING

Parenting is a learned behavior based on personal experiences and influenced by cultural beliefs. Individuals often implement parenting styles similar to their own parents' parenting styles. When investigating parenting techniques, researchers observe parent-child interactions, implement surveys, and conduct parent interviews. Observations and interviews focusing on parenting styles provide researchers with useful data and can identify generational patterns and cultural trends of parenting styles within identified demographics. To validate research on parenting styles, researchers implement consistent definitions to develop a common language. Diana Baumrind is a researcher who studied parent and child interaction. Baumrind's research dates back to 1967 and is considered foundational research regarding parenting. Baumrind's work identified specific parenting styles, and those parenting characteristics revealed parenting definitions that appear in research on parenting styles. Multiple parenting styles exist. Authoritative, authoritarian, and permissive parenting styles, however, serve as three foundational parenting-style frameworks for research projects that explore parenting influences on academic achievement and psychological development.

Three Major Parenting Styles

Authoritative

Brown and Shrinidhi (2008) explained that parents who implement authoritative parenting techniques establish rules and guidelines for children to follow. Authoritative parents are responsive and take time to explain family rules and guidelines to ensure understanding of the family expectations. According to Garcia and Garcia (2009), parents who undertake authoritative and nurturing practices are willing to listen to children's questions and attempt to answer the questions to develop understanding. Authoritative parents believe in a strong balance of discipline and love. Distinguished by a strategic combination of high warmth and firm control, the child and parent interaction is a priority in authoritative parenting methods. Authoritative parents engage in responsive dialogue with children to promote logic, and combine affection with punishment to promote positive self-concept. The combination of affection and punishment establishes a foundation for understanding discipline rather than penalizing discipline (De Lisi and Mcgillicuddy-De Lisi, 2007). Authoritative parents implement assertive, not restrictive, discipline to train and assist children in decision-making (Hermanns et al., 2008). Similar to authoritative parenting techniques, authoritarian parenting methods are firm and include specific guidelines. Authoritarian parents, however, do not implement the responsive dialogue applied by authoritative parents (Filiz & Yaprak, 2009).

Authoritarian

Authoritarian parents expect children to follow home rules established by parents without explanation or understanding (De Lisi and Mcgillicuddy-De Lisi). When children fail to follow the expected guidelines and rules, punitive punishment generally occurs. Discipline reminds children of the possible consequences of breaking rules. The goal is eliminating the behavior of disobeying established rules (De Lisi and Mcgillicuddy-De Lisi). Similar to authoritative parenting styles, authoritarian parents implement discipline to help children with future decision-making, but authoritative parents prioritize reasoning with children, and authoritarian parents prioritize authority and do not give attention to reasoning (Garcia & Garcia). Authoritarian parents want children to respect authority and understand the consequences of following established rules and guidelines (De Lisi and Mcgillicuddy-De Lisi). When children question rules and expectations, authoritarian parents generally refer to the expectation of obedience, point to parental authority, and demand adherence to rules without explaining the rationale for the rule or expectation (De Lisi and Mcgillicuddy-De Lisi). Authoritarian parents establish firm and explicit rules and are often intimidating to children (Brown & Shrinidhi). Authoritarian parents believe that children benefit from clear and explicit commands and regulations (Garcia & Martinez, 2008).

Authoritarian parenting styles generally produce obedient children, but rank lower in happiness, social competence, and self-esteem (De Lisi and Mcgillicuddy-De Lisi). The dictatorial techniques associated with authoritarian parenting styles significantly differ from permissive parenting techniques. Permissive parents prioritize having a friendly relationship with children and do not establish firm rules and regulations (Garcia & Martinez).

Permissive

Permissive parents, also referred to as indulgent parents, implement very few demands on children (De Lisi and Mcgillicuddy-De Lisi). Permissive parents focus on children enjoying childhood and have low expectations of maturity and self-control for children (De Lisi and Mcgillicuddy-De Lisi). According to Filiz and Yaprak (2009), permissive parents place high priority on being responsive to their children with the goal of establishing a relationship and positive self-concept. Parents who implement permissive techniques place few demands, inconsistent discipline, and lenient guidelines for children (Brown & Shrinidhi). Permissive parents value mercy toward children and seek to understand children's poor choices, rather than administering discipline and developing an awareness of dangers and consequences for poor choices (Filiz & Yaprak). According to Garcia and Garcia, permissive parents are commonly nurturing, talkative, and open with children; they create strong, responsive family environments. Parents implementing permissive techniques frequently assume the role of friends with children, rather than the status of authority (Brown & Shrinidhi).

Permissive parenting techniques commonly produce strong-willed children with healthy self-concepts, but lacking appropriate social skills in some environmental situations (Brown & Shrinidhi). The merciful and accommodating parenting style fosters habits in children that support self-interest and hinder the development of a cooperative attitude and self-discipline (Brown & Shrinidhi). School settings are examples of environmental situations where children of permissive parents lack appropriate social skills and regularly challenge rules and authority figures within the school system (De Lisi and Mcgillicuddy-De Lisi).

Benefits of Strategic Parenting

The discoveries of Smith (2008), Kennell (2006), and Milevsky et al. (2007) reveal authoritative parenting techniques foster an optimal environment that supports high self-esteem, complex thinking, and strong vocabulary development. Student achievement correlates with a child's ability to apply current knowledge to new information. Students' self-esteem influences their confidence and ability to transfer and apply current knowledge to unknown learning. According to Smith, authoritarian parenting techniques do not promote ongoing dialogue between parent and child and significantly limit the child's exposure to words. Smith explained that vocabulary is a reliable indicator of a child's academic success, and early development is essential to high achievement. Kennell linked parenting styles to the acquisition of knowledge and found authoritarian parenting techniques contribute to low attribution in students. According to Milevsky et al., authoritarian parenting techniques promote lower self-esteem and lower academic performance than non-authoritarian practices.

Parenting Styles and Epistemology

Kennell analyzed the influence parenting styles have on a child's epistemological beliefs. According to Bernardo (2007), epistemology is the theory of knowledge and describes an individual's ability to acquire new knowledge. Kennell explained that authoritative parenting techniques provide an environment in which parents encourage children to take responsibility in the home and positively support epistemology. According to Kennell, social relationships and responsive dialogue help form a child's epistemology belief. The purposeful communication and nurturing relationship in an authoritative home positively influence a child's ability to learn. Kennell's study, based on the epistemology theory of 2004, listed certain knowledge, simple knowledge, omniscient authority, quick learning, and innate learning as five ways individuals acquire knowledge. Kennell explained that students of authoritative parents were less likely to practice quick learning and had a strong understanding of the complex learning process. The study implemented two surveys using a Likert scale, one to assess parenting styles and one to determine the ability to acquire knowledge, or epistemology. The results of Kennell's study revealed that students with authoritative parents had the highest grade point average; students of authoritarian parents had the second highest; and students with uninvolved or permissive parents had the lowest grade point averages of the sampled students.

According to Kennell, authoritative parents believe that knowledge is complex and strive to strengthen learning through engaging children in dialogue. Prompting children to think before giving a response requires children to access prior learning to understand new concepts. Students nurtured in homes supporting self-regulation of learning and logical thinking display stronger cognitive skills (Brown & Shrinidhi). According to Kennell, permissive parents believe that knowledge is not sophisticated, and permissive parenting techniques do not foster childhood cognitive development. Permissive parents devote little attention to acquiring new learning strategies in children. According to Kennell, children cared for by authoritarian parents struggle with elaborating concepts and learning new things. Authoritarian parents, like authoritative parents, believe knowledge is complex, but authoritarian parents view the process of fostering knowledge as simple. Parents who implement authoritarian techniques do not equip students with the ability to implement learning strategies that foster logical thinking. Children of authoritarian parents often become frustrated in school environments because they have limited skills to engage in meaningful classroom discussions that promote new learning. Students nurtured in authoritarian, permissive, or authoritative homes can learn; however, the deficiency in logic skills that often accompanies students cared for in authoritarian and permissive homes requires additional instruction time and resources that assist students in learning. Students not exposed to responsive parenting environments at home often communicate simple answers to complex questions and appear intellectually lower than students who communicate complex questions with elaboration and logical understanding (Kennell). In examining the effects parenting has on academic performance, it is essential for educators to understand how parenting style influences student attribution.

Attribution theory describes an individual's personal view of the achievement of personal successes and failures and provides insight into intrinsic motivation. Individuals with high attribution view themselves mainly responsible for personal successes and see themselves as successful (Kennell). Persons with low attribution view success as dependent on outside factors and envision themselves as failures. A student's perception of him or herself influences interaction with others and affects the student's ability to ask appropriate questions; therefore, negative self-perception indirectly hinders students' academic achievement. According to Swinton (2008), adolescent student engagement is important to the development of sophisticated and complex thinking processes. Kennell explained that educators experience difficulty understanding the knowledge level of students who provide simple answers and nominal dialogue. These responses result in the educator having unclear knowledge of a student's academic ability. Students who ask questions, consistently engage in academic dialogue, and clearly articulate knowledge level promote positive interaction between student and teacher. Positive student and teacher interaction affirms students and assists in the development of high attribution in students (Kennell). According to Swinton, student and teacher interaction either positively or negatively influences student attribution as students begin to experience success or failure based on teacher affirmation.

Brown and Shrinidhi reported that authoritative parenting styles provide a stronger foundation for asking high-level questions and fostering higher attribution in students. Callahan and Eyberg (2009) explained that authoritarian parenting develops a minimal foundation for students to engage in higher-level questioning and fosters lower attribution in students. Parents who implement authoritarian parenting techniques focus on teaching family roles and following instruction given by authority figures. Authoritative parents prioritize reasoning and understanding, whereas authoritarian parents teach compliance. According to Chung and Rubin (2006), authoritarian parenting techniques do not promote high levels of knowledge acquisition. Chung and Rubin associated authoritarian parenting styles with negative outcomes in cognitive and social development of children and explained that authoritarian techniques negatively influence student achievement.

Parenting Styles and Vocabulary

Smith agreed that authoritarian techniques negatively contribute to student achievement. Smith explained that verbally engaged, visible, and active parents encourage high participation levels in classroom discussion and questioning that foster high literacy rates and strong cognitive understanding. Smith investigated how parenting styles influence vocabulary by selecting a random sample, and executed the study using mailed surveys, telephoned parenting surveys, and face-to-face interviews with parents. The study analyzed student vocabulary levels by examining Dynamic Indicators of Basic Early Learning Skills (DIBELS) assessments is—a reading assessment used to determine literacy and vocabulary development (Smith). Smith's study required pairing students' quantitative literacy scores with qualitative data collected from parent interviews and surveys, and provided data for the mixed-method correlational study. Smith investigated whether specific parenting styles correlated with stronger vocabulary scores. The results revealed that authoritative parents reported higher student reading achievement and vocabulary comprehension compared to other parenting styles. High-level, permissive parenting techniques represented students who fell significantly below grade level in reading and vocabulary skills.

According to Smith, authoritative parents implement responsive communication practices that expose students to rich vocabulary and language structure. Smith explained that reading activities and early exposure to conversations at home had a positive influence on reading comprehension, vocabulary development, and expressive language skills. Verhoven (2007) argued that responsive parent and child dialogue significantly increased the number of words in a child's vocabulary and assisted in strong reading comprehension. O'Neil-Pirozzi (2009) explained that children should actively engage in vocabulary-rich dialogue and participate in social experiences to acquire essential vocabulary and to develop strong reading comprehension and language skills. Without consistently experiencing responsive adult and child dialogue, a child's language suffers because of minimal exposure to words, which hinders academic achievement (Smith). Parenting styles that incorporate verbal engagement and responsiveness with a child create an environment conducive to language development and high student achievement (Girolametto & Weitzman, 2006). No other variable, including a parent's educational background or family's socioeconomic status, predicts vocabulary development more than the quantity of engaging conversation a parent and child encounter. Longest et al. (2008) explained that authoritative parents consistently engage in responsive dialogue with children and provide an optimal environment that assists developing strong cognitive and language skills.

Smith argued that authoritative parenting techniques support an active and communicative relationship that fosters high student achievement because of strong vocabulary development. Smith explained that parental interaction that affects a child's literacy practices has a more dominant influence on student achievement than any other family background variable, such as social class, level of parent's education, and family size. Bowen and Lee (2006) discussed the fact that certain parenting styles promote an environment that encourages more parent-child interaction than other parenting styles. Brooks-Gunn and

Markman (2005) explained that authoritative parenting techniques establish a foundation for strong language development during toddler age and vocabulary reasoning for school age, but authoritarian parenting styles teach hierarchy and authority and do not promote language and reasoning development. Longest et al. discussed the fact that numerous minority families implement authoritarian parenting styles and do not provide optimal environments that support strong vocabulary, which could contribute to the gap in academic performance among minority and non-minority students. The development of language contributes to academic achievement, and parenting styles influence the development of language.

Children not consistently engaged in responsive adult and child dialogue receive less exposure to words than those who are which results in a possible academic performance discrepancy indirectly associated to parenting styles because of limited vocabulary development (Bowen & Lee). Students nurtured in homes with authoritarian parenting characteristics generally have lower expressive language, and do not have opportunities to engage in meaningful dialogue at home. The expressive-language deficit transfers to the classroom and contributes to communication-skill differences among students nurtured in authoritative homes and students cared for in non-authoritative homes (Brooks-Gunn & Markman). Riddell and Stojansvik (2008) explained that receptive language is the ability to understand and comprehend statements, and expressive language is the ability to use words to express thought. Expressive language is important to a student's academic success because of the ability to articulate cognitive understanding (Betts, 2008). School districts often assess expressive language and analyze results for student placement into challenging academic programs (Harris et al., 2009).

According to Betts, practicing receptive language involves less cognitive ability than implementing expressive language. Children of authoritarian parents receive practice in receptive language because of the commands often given to children; however, minimal opportunities for self-expression or expression of thought exist because of nominal responsive communication (Smith). Authoritarian parenting techniques teach children to obey guidelines, and the strategy includes minimal discussion between parent and child. Authoritarian parenting styles do not encourage children to reason, express mental thought, or ask questions; therefore, children in authoritarian homes receive minimal opportunities to practice expressive language. Minimizing expressive communication hinders a child's academic development and supports low student academic performance (Chung & Rubin).

Parenting Styles and Self-Esteem

Milevsky, Keehn, Netter, and Schlechter (2007) conducted a qualitative study to analyze the influence parenting style has on adolescent self-esteem. Information from the study revealed the authoritarian parenting style supports a type of relationship that contributes to low self-esteem in children (Milevsky et al.). This parenting approach to child rearing produces compliant children who practice limited thinking for themselves and excel in following directives and commands from authority (Milevsky et al.). Parents who employ non-authoritative techniques do not prioritize teaching personal responsibility and decision-making to children; this offers minimal opportunity for children to experience individual accomplishments, fostering low self-confidence (Milevsky et al.). The analysis of data collected in the study used multivariate analysis of variance (MANOVA), with parenting style and gender being the independent variable and self-esteem and depression being the dependent variable. The study results revealed that adolescent children nurtured in authoritarian parenting techniques were more likely to have low self-confidence and suffer from depression than adolescent children cared for in other parenting environments (Milevsky et al.).

According to Hill (1995), authoritative parenting styles encourage independent thinking and self-directed behavior. Children who practice independent thinking and personal decision-making often are confident and have positive self-worth, high attribution, and high student achievement (Hill). According to Mehay and Pema (2009), a child with a strong sense of self-worth is more capable of solving problems independently and answering complex questions. DeHart, Pelham, and Tennen (2006) found that adults who had nurturing parents reported higher self-esteem than adults whose parents were less nurturing. According to Callahan and Eyberg (2009), permissive and authoritarian parenting styles create low self-esteem in children, whereas authoritative parenting styles encourage strong self-concept. Antonio and Patock-Peckham (2009) found that authoritative parenting techniques promote better social skills, academic success, and higher degrees of self-regulation.

Parents should understand that parenting styles are generally situational and most parents implement all three types of styles at some point when interacting with children. Parents also need to be aware that individuals most likely have a default parenting style and usually have a dominate strategy. Because some parenting techniques provide more language development than other parenting strategies, parents need to be mindful of their parent and child interaction. When parents understand the type of parenting styles and the influences the styles have on a child's success, they are empowered to practice strategic interaction.

THE POWER OF STRATEGIC INTERACTION

Brain research supports the importance of strategic parenting techniques in regards to cognitive development and student achievement. The quality of interaction between a child and his or her primary caregiver has a decisive influence on how the brain develops. Brain development continues after birth and grows most quickly during the early years of life. Parents who engage their children in dialogue and questioning create an atmosphere that promotes healthy and strong brain development. Children who do not have a home atmosphere that promotes language and dialogue are hindered. Research shows a rich vocabulary and verbal interaction dramatically influences school readiness and student academic achievement. Reading is like a dance between the print on the page and the knowledge in your mind. Words come alive and obtain meaning based on your previous exposure and understanding of language. Having a strong vocabulary and language skills assist with reading because children can use their known words and knowledge to interact with the print on the page and quickly develop meaning. When a good reader encounters an unfamiliar word, he or she stops to analyze the word, which slows down reading fluency and hinders comprehension. Eye-movement research reveals that readers look at every word and almost every letter of each word to determine meaning of the letters and words. Familiar words are instantly recognized and processed as eye movement occurs.

Recognizing a word visually is the quickest form of word recognition and discerning meaning; however, recognizing a word that has been heard before provides a mental bank that supports quick word recognition that strengthens fluency and developing meaning. Unfamiliar words interfere with reading comprehension. Good readers' processing time is shorter than poor readers' processing time because most good readers had exposure to many words and they use those words when reading. This allows an individual the ability to recognize words quicker and fosters strong reading comprehension. The more accustomed an individual is to words, the better the reading comprehension. Reading comprehension has a direct influence on academic achievement in all educational areas.

Successful strategic parenting includes some characteristics of authoritative parenting techniques. Authoritative parenting cultivates an atmosphere that fosters strong language development. It also creates an environment for healthy and academically rich brain development. According to Garcia and Garcia (2009), parents who practice authoritative practices are willing to listen to children's questions and attempt to answer the questions to develop understanding. Authoritative parents believe in a strong balance of discipline and love. Distinguished by a strategic combination of high warmth and firm control, the child and parent interaction is a priority (Garcia &Martinez, 2008). Authoritative parents engage in responsive dialogue with children to promote logic and they combine affection with punishment to promote positive self-concept. Children nurtured in homes with high level of authoritative techniques have stronger vocabulary and higher self-confidence than children nurtured in homes with low levels of authoritative parenting.

Not only does poor parenting interaction create poor language development, but also it also negatively affects the brain's ability to develop. The human body is born with 100 billion neurons that make connections through synapses, informally known as "wiring." An individual's experiences influence the nature and quantity of synaptic connections. Because the brain functions on a "use it or lose it" code, some connections are fostered and others hindered. Only the connections and pathways commonly used are activated and retained. Connections not consistently used are removed. With the discarding of the inactive connections, the active connections become more prevalent and stronger in the brain. Children are born ready to learn, but their life experiences determine how much learning occurs. According to Edie and Schmid (2007), children cultivate 85 percent of their intelligence, personality, and talents by age five. Recognizing that fact, parents need to understand kindergarten does not mark the beginning of academic learning. It is not the environment where the stage of learning begins. The initial years of life set the stage for lifelong learning and the majority of those years are spent with the primary caregiver and day-care facilities. Edie and Schmid (2007) explained research in brain development reveals four important elements, which are as follow:

1. The manner in which the brain develops depends on the interplay between the genetic material a person is born with and the life experiences a person encounters from birth.
2. It takes up to twelve years for the brain to organize, with parts of the frontal cortex not developing until the early twenties.
3. The quality of an infant's relationship with his or her primary caregivers has a significant influence on the structural design of the brain, affecting the nature and extent of various capabilities later in life.
4. Early interactions affect the development design of the brain.

Repeated experiences are necessary for children's brains to become highly developed. Large amounts of synaptic connections make the brain stronger, more efficient, and ready for academic learning. Reading to children every day and providing opportunities to practice social skills and responsive conversation with adults provide opportunities to develop both large- and small-muscle skills in the brain. Edie and Schmid explained, "It is vital to incorporate rich language into all parent and child interactive activities, since exposure to rich language creates the foundation for a child's usage and understanding of words. This foundation increases the likelihood of reading success at a later age. There is an urgent need for the families to engage in reflective discussions regarding the role of parenting and the implications various parenting styles have on a child's success in life.

PARENTING IN ACTION

The following story chronicles the interaction between two mothers and their daughters. One of the mothers implements strategic interaction that fosters dialogue in the home. Although the other mother has positive interaction with her child, she does not implement a parenting style that promotes parent and child conversation. Read the passage below, reflecting on the parent and child interaction and the influence that interaction has on their child's educational experience.

The Story of Cassandra and Stephanie

Cassandra sat wide-eyed looking at the red and orange blaze. She loved the way the colors seemed to sparkle right before her eyes. The warmth from the fire intrigued her and seemed to call her to come closer. As Cassandra started to walk closer to the fire, she looked over her left shoulder and locked eyes with the female adult standing behind her.

"I told you not to get close to that fire, Cassandra!" the feminine voice said firmly.

"Why can't I get close?" Cassandra questioned.

"Because I said so, Cassandra," Cassandra's mother answered. "Do not ask my why, just do what I ask you to do," Cassandra's mother stated as she locked eyes with Cassandra.

Cassandra quickly stepped back from the fireplace and watched her mother close the fireplace screen.

Stephanie could not believe something so beautiful could be so destructive. She loved to watch the fire flicker in the fireplace and enjoyed the red and orange colors dance before her eyes. The warmth was welcoming, but the beauty did not fool her. She knew the danger.

"Remember what I told you Stephanie," her mother said firmly.

"I remember, don't get to close to the fire," Stephanie recited in the same tone her mother told her.

"That's right, fire is dangerous, don't let the beauty fool you," Stephanie's mother confirmed.

"Fire can and will burn almost everything it touches." Her mother said.

"I know mom, you don't have to remind me," Stephanie whined.

"Okay, because it will burn your hand, just like it destroyed that house on the news last night," Her mother stated firmly.

Stephanie remembered the black ashes that covered the remains of the red house that caught on fire last night near downtown. As she remembered the woman crying about losing everything on the television news, Stephanie stepped back from the fireplace.

The interaction between the two little girls and their moms is an example of the type of the on going interaction between the mothers and daughters. The situation regarding the fire is just one example of how the mothers responded to expectations of rules and the manner in which they explained questions posed by their daughters.

Two years have pass and Stephanie and Cassandra are preparing to start kindergarten. As they get ready for the first day of school, both girls are nervous and have many questions. As Stephanie puts on her jacket, she asks her mother for the fifth time "What if no one likes me and I don't make any friends."

Stephanie's mother took a deep breath to hide her frustration and stated "Stephanie, why do you think no one is going to like you?"

"Because they may not like my clothes or they may think my name is funny," Stephanie said with tears in her eyes.

"Stephanie," her mother said with pride in her voice. "Do you not know what your name means?" Stephanie looked puzzled.

"No, mom," I didn't even know names had meanings," Stephanie stated with a confused tone.

"Every name has a meaning and the name Stephanie means crown."

"You mean like Cinderella?" Stephanie questioned.

"Exactly, but better because you can never take this

crown off. It is in your name and you can't take your name off, can you?" Stephanie's mother asked with a smile.

"No, mom that is silly. No one can take off their name." Stephanie said with confidence.

"Well, since your name means crown and you can not take off your name, you are a full time princess. If someone makes fun of you or your name then they must not know who you are, because no one makes fun of a princess." Her mother reassured.

"You right, mom, do I tell them that I am a princess." Stephanie wondered.

"Not yet, there may come a time when we have to tell, Stephanie's mother stated.

"Okay," Stephanie said with pride.

"Everyday after school, you tell me what happened at school; then we can discuss if it is time to tell the others that you are a princess," Her mother said with a smile.

"I like that," Stephanie added. As they got in the car, Stephanie thought about the princess secret. She looked forward to the first day of school, but was more excited about the after school talks with her mom.

"Cassandra, are you excited about your first day of school?" Cassandra's mother asked.

"Yes, I think."

"You think?" Cassandra's mother questioned, with a smile. "You should know if you are excited or not."

"Yes, I am."

"That is great, I am proud of you and I bet you will be the smartest student in class" Cassandra's mother stated with confidence.

"Do you think?" Cassandra asked.

"Oh, I know you will show everyone that you are smart. Be sure you listen to the teacher and do what she tells you to do." Her mother added. "It is important that you obey the teacher and not be disrespectful to any adults in your school."

"Yes, mama," Cassandra said with clear understanding of what her mother meant. Cassandra knew that if she got in trouble at school for not be respectful to her teacher or other adults, she would get in trouble at home."

"Now, let's get to our first day of school,"

Stephanie and Cassandra are excited about starting school and eager to learn new things and make friends. Although, they are enrolled in the same school, share the same classroom, and have the same teacher, Stephanie and Cassandra's are about to start an academic journey that is very different from the other. The first day of kindergarten offered different experiences for the two girls and the contrasting academic experience continued throughout most of their academic careers.

Stephanie and Cassandra sat anxiously at the kindergarten tables, as their teacher instructed them about the classroom rules and expectations. Stephanie was sitting at the red table and Cassandra assigned to the green table. All the children in the classroom liked their colored table and enjoyed looking at all the pictures on the walls; Stephanie and Cassandra were not exception.

"All right boys and girls, it is story time." Mrs. Icy, the kindergarten teacher said. The students sat on the carpet, as Mrs. Icy prepared to read her class a story. The teacher held up the book and displayed the pictures as she read the story about the boys going on a camping trip. The children watched and listened totally engaged in Mrs. Icy's animated voice and the beautiful pictures in the book.

"Who knows what this picture is," Mrs. Icy asked the class.

Almost all the students raised their hands, and Stephanie and Cassandra raised their hands as well. The teacher called on Cassandra.

"It is a picture of fire!" Cassandra answered confidently.

"That is correct, Cassandra," Mrs. Icy responded. "What do you know about fire?" The kindergarten teacher asked her.

"You don't touch it!" Cassandra answered proudly; as she attempted to demonstrate, she was the smartest student in the classroom.

"Very good, Cassandra," Mrs. Icy stated, "Who else can tell me something about fire?"

Stephanie was almost out of her seat when Mrs. Icy called her to answer." Fire is dangerous, it can burn almost anything it touches, it burns houses and takes away people things, and you should not be fooled by its beauty."

"Oh, my Stephanie, what an informative answer, you sure do know a great deal about fire." Mrs. Icy stated with happiness in her voice. She was excited because it appeared that Stephanie might be a smart student in her classroom, and all teachers like to have smart students. Cassandra looked at Stephanie with aspiration and wondered if Stephanie was smarter than she was. Cassandra looked at Mrs. Icy and noticed she was pleased with Stephanie. Stephanie looked at the teacher and told herself that she would be sure to tell her mother that the teacher liked her.

As the students were taking their naps after lunch recess, Mrs. Icy took the time to take observational notes on the students in her assessment notebook. The assessment notebook helped Mrs. Icy and the other teachers indentify students who may need additional support in learning. As she wrote in her notebook, she came to Stephanie's name and recorded the words verbal, good vocabulary, and smart. She later came to Cassandra's name in her notebook and wrote the words behaved, willing to answer questions, and may need intervention. Mrs. Icy placed a star beside Cassandra's name to remind her to pay close attention to Cassandra for additional academic support.

The story of Stephanie and Cassandra are similar because both tell a story concerning a little girl interacting with her mother and the influence that interaction had on the girls' schoolings. Both mothers desired compliance, because neither wanted their daughter to get too close to the fire in the fireplace. Although both mothers wanted the same outcome, they had different methods and reasoning for achieving the goal. Cassandra's mother wanted Cassandra to respect her position as the parent, obey her authority, and not touch the fire. Stephanie's mother wanted her to understand the danger of fire, have the ability to realize that is the best choice, and not touch the fire. Both mothers expect obedience from their children.

At the beginning of every year, several kindergarten teachers complete some form of kindergarten evaluation and the assessments is oftentimes observational. The teachers observe students behavior as they interact with others and the classroom environment. The kindergarten teachers take notes about student's behavior and documents academic concerns. Mrs. Icy, like so many other kindergarten teachers, formed an opinion on Stephanie and Cassandra's intelligence based on the girls' interaction within the classroom setting. Mrs. Icy did not say that Cassandra was not intelligent, but she did recognize her as a student who may require additional academic support. Cassandra will have additional opportunities to display her intelligence, but will not verbally express a clear understanding of mastery of academic learning in the classroom.

Which parent implemented strategic interaction and did the interaction give her daughter and academic edge? What is your parenting style? Do you provide your child an academic edge? Does your interaction with your children establish a foundation for the school system to expand your child's learning? Who is your child's first teacher? Are you being bailed out? Hopefully, you have been reflecting on your parenting behavior as you have been reading this book. Do you know your dominate parenting style yet? I say dominate parenting style, because most parents implement all styles at some point in time. The situation often guides behavior. In the next chapter you will have the opportunity to take a quiz that will assist you in determining your dominate parenting style. There are no right or wrong answers for the quiz; it is simply a tool to guide you during self reflection.

WHAT IS YOUR PARENTING STYLE?

Instructions: For each of the following statements, circle the number of the 5-point scale (1 = *strongly disagree*, 5 = *strongly agree*) that best describes how that statement applies to your perception of parenting. Try to read and think about each statement as it applies to you and your interaction with your children. There is no right or wrong answer, so just answer as best you can.

1. As my children were growing up, I directed their activities and decisions through reasoning and discipline.

   1   2   3   4   5

2. Children need to have freedom to make up their mind and do what they want.

   1   2   3   4   5

3. Once family rules are established, I do not mind discussing the reasoning behind the policy with the children.

    1   2   3   4   5

4. I let my children know what I expect of them and it upsets me if they try to disagree with me

    1   2   3   4   5

5. I seldom give my children a list of expectations, I want them to discover and have the freedom to learn on their own.

    1   2   3   4   5

6. If my child does not meet the expectations I have established, I let them know with I expect and punish them.

    1   2   3   4   5

7. Children should have the opportunity to have their way just like parents.

    1   2   3   4   5

8. I generally give my children direction and guid-
   ance in rational and objective ways and welcome
   questions.

   1   2   3   4   5

9. I expect my children to conform to my expectations out of respect for my authority.

   1   2   3   4   5

10. When children do not agree with family rules, I
    feel it is best for them if they conform to the rules
    regardless of their opinions.

    1   2   3   4   5

11. I desire to be my child's friend and am careful not
    to hurt that relationship.

    1   2   3   4   5

12. Most of the time, I do what the children want to
    do.

    1   2   3   4   5

13. I give my children clear expectations, but I under-
    stand and allow them to disagree.

    1   2   3   4   5

14. I consider my children's opinion when making decisions, but their opinions do not guide the decisions.

    1   2   3   4   5

15. If parents would focus on getting their children to behave and follow authority, the society would be better.

    1   2   3   4   5

Add the value of your answers in the following manner:

A _____ (numbers 1, 3, 8, 13, and 14)
B _____ (numbers 2, 5, 7, 11, and 12)
C _____ (numbers 4, 6, 9, 10, and 15)

A= is the highest number *authoritative* is likely your dominant style.

B=is the highest number *permissive* is likely your dominant style

C= is the highest number *authoritarian* is likely your dominant style

NECESSARY CONVERSATIONS

Similar to my first book title, *Because I Said So: A Discussion on Parenting Styles and Achievement Gaps,* this book is designed to start necessary discussions. The questions listed below are designed to prompt honest and necessary conversations among Americans. The answers to the questions will come from collective and sincere conversations regarding our families, school systems, and society.

1. What do you think is the core root to the anger and frustration found in so many Americans today?
2. Do you believe a successful society needs to function as functionalists believe and support the various social systems to ensure success for all social systems?
3. Why do you think bank and corporate bailouts are unaccepted, but parent bailouts are expected?
4. How would you define the term "parent bailout" and do you think the term has validity?
5. Do you think the current school systems function in their intended purpose?
6. In your opinion, which do you think is more

damaging to a society: failing families or failing private businesses?

7. Do you think failing schools are a result of failing families and "big government"?

8. Is there a correlation between "big government" and the weakening of other social systems?

9. What do you think is a foundational piece to a strong family?

10. What do you think is a foundational piece to a strong school system?

My prayer is that these questions prompt healthy and necessary conversations that will drive discussions within our society to strengthen all social systems. Anger just divides people if it does not prompt strategic action to solve the problem. We are a "united" America that is built on a foundation of strong families, healthy government, successful businesses, churches that seek truth, and an effective health care system. Although each social system is very different and has its own defined part, all social systems must work together in order for our country to become the civilization we desire. Necessary conversations are critical, because the failure of one social system will mean failure for them all.

Although all social systems are important, the family social system serves as a foundational structure. The failure of the family negatively affects other social systems. Therefore, strengthening the family will positively influence multiple social systems. Like education, the family structure is complex. But, understanding the implications of the various parent and child interaction is one manner in which families can examine their health and respond accordingly. Are you permissive, authoritative, or authoritarian? Do you know the affects of your parent and child interaction? Are they positive or negative? Are you a parent that needs a bailout? Do you know a parent that the school has to bailout? Do not be fooled and think that the school bailing out someone else does not affect you. If the schools are occupied with parenting other people's kids, then who is instructing your child?

Bailouts are not new and have a necessary role in a successful society. Although bailouts provide a system for the success of all social structures, it is essential that they are balanced. Balancing occurs when the amount of support is monitored. Monitoring the support one social system gives another establishes an atomosphere that decreases the danger of minimizing one social structure and exhausting the other.

Do you think monitoring the non-academic support schools give to families would strengthen schools? Go through the discussion questions with someone.Get involved in your local community, because the answer to struggling schools starts with us

REFERENCES

Alexander, P., Knudson, R., Quirk, M., & Zitzer-Comfort, C. (2008). The California State University early assessment program. *The Clearing House, 81*(5), 227-231.

Antonio, A. & Patock-Peckham, J. (2009). Meditational links among parenting styles, perceptions of parental confidence, self-esteem, and depression on alcohol-related problems in emerging adulthood. *Journal of Studies on Alcohol and Drugs, 70*(2), 215.

Ascher, C. & Maguire, C. (2007). Beating the odds. *Annenberg Institute for School Reform.* Brown University. Retrieved from http://www.annenberginstitute.org

Ashagre, Y. & Donald, A. (2007). Dynamic analysis of income and independence effect of African American female labor force participation on divorce. *Atlantic Economic Journal, 35*(2), 159-171. Doi 10.1007/s11293-006-9059-1.

Bates, J., Deater-Deckard, K., Dodge, K., & Pettit, G. (1996). Physical discipline among African American and European American mothers: Links to children's externalizing behaviors *Developmental Psychology, 32*, 1065-1072.

Battle, A. (2009). *The relationship between major field of study and teacher dispositions of student success.*

Baumrind, D. (1967). Childcare practices anteceding three patterns of preschool behavior. *Genetic Psychology Monographs, 75*(1), 43-88.

Bernardo, A. (2008). Exploring epistemological beliefs of bilingual Filipino pre-service teachers in the Filipino and English languages. *Journal of Psychology.*

Betts, D. (2008). *Exploring the relationship between language and reading skills and Ohio Graduation Test performance.*

Bluman, A. (2009). *Elementary statistics: A step-by-step approach.* New York, NY: Irwin Professional Publishing.

Blumenthal, R. (2006). Why Connecticut sued the federal government over No Child Left Behind. *Harvard Educational Review, 76*(4), 564-569,725.

Boulter, D. (2008). *Family structure and adolescent delinquency: Examining the influence of parenting and extended family support.*

Bowen, N. & Lee, J., (2006). Parent involvement, cultural capital, and the achievement gap among elementary school children. *American Educational Research Journal, 43*(2), 193-218.

Bradshaw, C., Hershfeldt, P., Leaf, P., & Pas, E. (2010). A multilevel exploration of the influence of teacher efficacy and burnout on response to student problem behavior and school-based service use. *School Psychology Quarterly, 25*(1), 13-27. Doi: 10.1037/a0018576

Brooks-Gunn, J., & Markman, L B (2005). The contribution of parenting to ethnic and racial gaps in school readiness. *The Future of Children, 15*(1) p.139.

Retrieved www.rch.org.au/ccch/policybriefs.cfm

Brown, L. & Shrinidhi, I. (2008). Parenting styles: the impact on student achievement. *Marriage and Family Review, 43*(1/2), 14-38.

Buri, J. (1991). Parental Authority Questionnaire. *Journal of Personality Assessment, 57*(1), 110.

Bushaw, W., Ferriter, B., Finn, C., Gallup, A., Hammond, D., Merrow, J., & Tucker, L. (2008). Americans speak out – are educators and policy makers listening? *Phi Delta Kappan, 90*(1), 9-20.

Callahan, C.L., & Eyberg, S.M. (2009). Relations between parenting behavior and SES in a clinical sample: Validity of SES measures. *Child & Family Behavior Therapy.* Retrieved EBSCOhost database. Doi: 10.1016/S0924-9338(09)70861-2

Chung, O. & Rubin, K. (2006). *Parenting beliefs, behaviors, and parent-child relations: A cross-cultural perspective.* New York, NY: Taylor and Francis Group.

Creswell, J. W. (2005). *Educational research: planning, conducting, and evaluating quantitative and qualitative research.* Upper Saddle River: Pearson

De Lisi, R., and Mcgillicuddy-De Lisi, A. (2007). Perceptions of family relations when mothers and fathers are depicted with different parenting styles. *Journal of Genetic Psychology*, 168, 4. p.425 (18).

DeHart, T., Pelham, B., & Tennen, H. (2006). What lies beneath: Parenting style and implicit self-esteem. *Journal of Experimental Social Psychology, 42*(1), 1-17.

DeMarrais, K., & LeCompte, M. (1999). *The way schools work: A sociological analysis of education* (3rd ed.). New York, NY: Windridge.

Dorn, L. & Soffos, C. (2006). *Teaching for deeper comprehension*. Portland, ME: Steinhouse Publishers.

Ekman, P. (2009). *Emotions revealed: Recognizing faces and feelings to improve communication emotional life*. St. Manhattan, NY: Henry Holt and Company.

Filiz, Z. & Yaprak, B. (2009). A study of classifying parenting styles through discriminate analysis. Journal of Theory and Practice in Education, 5(2), 197-209.

Foote, M. (2009). Stepping out of the classroom: Building teacher knowledge for developing classroom practices. *Teacher Education Quarterly, 36*(3), 39-54

Garcia, E., & Garcia, F. (2009). Is always authoritative the optimum parenting style? Evidence from Spanish families. *Adolescence, 44*, 173.

Garcia, J., & Martinez, I. (2008). Internalization of values and self-esteem among Brazilian teenagers from authoritative, indulgent, authoritarian, and neglectful homes. *Adolescence, 43*, 169.

Geisler, J., Hessler, T., Gardner, R., & Lovelace, T. (2009). Differentiated writing interventions for high-achieving urban African American elementary students. *Journal of Advanced Academics, 20*(2), 214-247,369-371.

Gilkman, C. (2008). The latest nation at risk report. *The forum of education and democracy.* Retrieved from hoover.org/publications/policy review/3563967.html

Girolametto, L. & Weitzman, E. (2006). It Takes Two to Talk - The Hanen Program for Parents: Early Language Intervention through Caregiver Training. In R. McCauley and M. Fey (Eds.), *Treatment of language disorders in children,* pp. 77-103. New York: Brookes Publishing.

Greif, A. (2006). Family structure, institutions, and growth: The origins and implications of western corporations. *American Economic Review, 96*(2), 308-312.

Grothaus, T. & Schellenberg, R. (2009). Promoting cultural responsiveness and closing the achievement gap with standards blending. *Professional School Counseling, 12*(6), 440-449.

Harris, B., Martinez, R., Plucker, J., & Rapp, K. (2009). Identifying gifted and talented English language learners: A case study. *Journal for the Education of the Gifted, 32*(3), 368-393.

Hathorn, P. (2005). Effective literacy education for the inner city African American male: Key elements of a technology-based program. Ed.D. dissertation, University of California, Berkeley, CA.

Hui-Chin, H. & Jihyun, S. (2009). *International Journal of Behavioral Development, 33*(5), 430-439.

Kennell, B. L. (2006). *The relationship between parenting style and epistemological beliefs.*

Latshaw, C., Papamarcos, S., & Watson, G. (2007). Individualism-collectivism and incentive system design as predictive of productivity in a simulated cellular manufacturing environment. *International Journal of Cross Cultural Management: CCM, 7*(2), 253-265.

Longest, K. Taylor, L., Barnett, M. & Raver,C. (2008). Parenting styles in African American and white low-income families. The Annual Meeting of the American Sociological Association. http://www.allacademic.com/meta/p183722

Lynch, J. (2010). Kindergarten teachers' beliefs about students' knowledge of print literacy and parental involvement in children's print literacy development. *Alberta Journal of Educational Research*, 56(2), 157-171.

Maddox, A. (2009). Politics of *Brown v. Board of Education*. *New York Amsterdam News, 100*(20), 12-14.

Mason, B., Temple-Harvey, K., & Vannest, K. (2009). Adequate yearly progress for students with emotional and behavioral disorders through research-based practices. *Preventing School Failure, 53*(2), 73-83.

Mehay, S. & Pema, E. (2009). The effect of high school JROTC on student achievement, educational attainment, and enlistment. *Southern Economic Journal, 76*(2), 533-552.

Mercer, V., Hankins, C., Spinks, A., & Tedder, D. (2009). Reliability and validity of a clinical test of reaction time in older adults. *Journal of Geriatric Physical Therapy, 32*(3), 103-110.

Milevsky, A., Keehn, D., Netter, S., & Schlechter, M., (2007). Maternal and paternal parenting styles in adolescents: Associations with self-esteem, depression, and life-satisfaction. *Journal of Child and Family Studies, 16*(1), 39.

Miners, R. (2001). Parenting style, moral development, and friendship: How do we choose our friends? M.A. dissertation, Concordia University (Canada), Canada.

Murphy, M. (2006). *The history and philosophy of education: Voices of educational pioneers*. Prentice Hall, Inc.

O'Neil-Pirozzi, T. (2009). Feasibility and benefit of parent participation in a program emphasizing preschool child language development while homeless. *American Journal of Speech - Language Pathology, 18*(3), 252-63.

Riddell, P., & Stojansvik, V. (2008). Expressive versus

receptive language skills in specific reading disorder. *Clinical Linguistics Phonetics, 22*(4), 305-310.

Shanklin, N. (2007). What is this new emphasis on vocabulary all about? *Voices from the Middle, 15*(1), 52-53.

Shore, B. (2009). Making time for family: Schemas for long-term family memory. *Social Indicators Research, 93*(1), 95-103.

Smalls, C. (2007). *Self-regulation in the classroom and beyond: The roles of parenting practices, racial socialization, and racial identity in African American youth.*

Smith, T. (2008). *An examination of parental involvement factor on reading achievement scores in an inner city school.*

Solomon, D. (2007). As states tackle poverty, preschool gets high marks. *The Wall Street Journal, 65*(2)7-13.

Thijs, J., & Verkuyten, M. (2009). Students' anticipated situational engagement: The roles of teacher behavior, personal engagement, and gender. *The Journal of Genetic Psychology, 170*(3), 268-286.

Verhoven, M. (2007). Parenting during toddlerhood contributions of parental, contextual, and child characteristic. *Journal of Family Issues, 28*(12), 1663-1691.